AMANPREET KAUR

The Ultimate Guide to Excelling in PTE

A Step-by-Step Guide to Top Scores

Rana Books

First published by Rana Books Uk 2023

First edition

Contents

Foreword

I am thrilled to present "The Ultimate Guide to Excelling in PTE: A Step-by-Step Guide to Top Scores," an invaluable resource for individuals aiming to achieve outstanding results in the PTE exam. As the CEO and Founder of Rana Books, it gives me great pleasure to endorse this comprehensive guide that is meticulously designed to empower test-takers on their journey to success.

Preparing for the PTE exam can be a challenging endeavor, and I have personally witnessed the struggles that individuals face in their pursuit of excellence. This guide, however, is a game-changer. It offers a step-by-step approach that unravels the intricacies of the PTE exam, equipping test-takers with the knowledge, strategies, and practice materials needed to surpass their goals.

"The Ultimate Guide to Excelling in PTE" sets the stage for success by providing a solid foundation. From understanding the exam structure and scoring criteria to developing personalized study plans, this guide ensures that test-takers are equipped with the essential tools to excel.

What sets this guide apart is its in-depth focus on honing the specific skills required in each section of the PTE exam. Whether it is improving speaking fluency and pronunciation, mastering listening comprehension, enhancing reading speed and comprehension, or crafting well-structured written responses, this guide provides a wealth of expert guidance, practical tips, and targeted exercises to help test-takers elevate their performance.

In addition to skill development, the guide emphasizes the importance of test-taking strategies and time management. It equips test-takers with the necessary techniques to optimize their performance, make effective use of time constraints, and approach the exam with confidence and clarity.

I am impressed by the inclusion of mock tests and practice exercises, allowing test-takers to simulate the exam environment and gain valuable insights into their strengths and areas for improvement. Furthermore, the appendix, featuring a PTE score conversion table, sample scored responses, and detailed explanations, provides invaluable resources that enhance understanding and facilitate self-assessment.

I extend my heartfelt congratulations to the author for her meticulous work in creating this exceptional guide. "The Ultimate Guide to Excelling in PTE" will undoubtedly be an indispensable companion for all individuals striving to achieve top scores in the PTE exam.

I wholeheartedly endorse this guide and encourage all test-takers to seize this opportunity to unlock their full potential and embark on a journey to PTE success. Prepare with confidence, follow the step-by-step guidance, and celebrate your achievements as you excel in the PTE exam.

Best regards,

Ranjot Singh Chahal
CEO & Founder of Rana Books

Preface

Welcome to "The Ultimate Guide to Excelling in PTE: A Step-by-Step Guide to Top Scores." This book has been meticulously crafted to provide test-takers like you with a comprehensive resource that will help you achieve exceptional scores in the PTE exam. Whether you are just beginning your PTE preparation journey or seeking to improve your existing skills, this guide is designed to equip you with the knowledge, strategies, and practice materials necessary for success.

As the demand for English language proficiency assessments continues to grow, the Pearson Test of English (PTE) has emerged as a popular choice among test-takers worldwide. Recognizing the significance of this exam in your academic and professional pursuits, we have dedicated ourselves to creating a guide that addresses the unique challenges posed by the PTE and guides you toward achieving your desired scores.

"The Ultimate Guide to Excelling in PTE" takes a step-by-step approach, ensuring that you have a solid foundation to build upon throughout your preparation. We start by providing a comprehensive overview of the exam structure and scoring criteria, giving you a clear understanding of what to expect. We then guide you in setting realistic goals, developing effective study plans, and optimizing your preparation time.

Each section of the PTE exam is covered in detail, with a focus on the specific skills required to excel in speaking, listening, reading, and writing. From enhancing your pronunciation and fluency to sharpening your comprehension and response-building abilities, we provide expert guidance, practical tips, and ample practice exercises to hone your skills.

Furthermore, we understand that test-taking strategies and time management are crucial factors in achieving top scores. That is why we have dedicated sections to equip you with valuable techniques to approach each section with confidence and maximize your performance under timed conditions.

Throughout this guide, you will find mock tests and practice drills that simulate the actual exam experience. These exercises not only help you familiarize yourself with the exam format but also allow you to assess your progress and identify areas for improvement. The included appendix features a PTE score conversion table, sample scored responses, and detailed explanations, providing you with valuable insights into the scoring process and helping you gauge your performance effectively.

It is our sincere hope that "The Ultimate Guide to Excelling in PTE" will serve as your trusted companion on your PTE preparation journey. We have poured our knowledge, expertise, and passion into creating this guide, and we are confident that it will empower you to achieve your desired scores and unlock new opportunities in your educational and professional endeavors.

We would like to express our gratitude to all the individuals who have contributed to the creation of this guide, including educators, experts, and the dedicated team at Rana Books. We would also like to extend our appreciation to the readers and test-takers who have placed their trust in this resource.

Now, let's embark on this journey together and pave the way for your success in the PTE exam. With dedication, perseverance, and the guidance provided in this guide, you are well on your way to achieving top scores in the PTE.

Best wishes,

Amanpreet Kaur
Author

Acknowledgement

I would like to express my heartfelt gratitude to all those who have contributed to the creation of "The Ultimate Guide to Excelling in PTE: A Step-by-Step Guide to Top Scores." This book has been a labor of love, and I am grateful for the support, guidance, and inspiration I have received throughout this journey.

First and foremost, I would like to extend my deepest appreciation to my family and friends for their unwavering support and encouragement. Your belief in me and your constant motivation have been instrumental in bringing this project to fruition.

I would like to express my sincere thanks to my mentor and advisors, whose expertise and guidance have been invaluable. Your insights and constructive feedback have played a crucial role in shaping this guide and ensuring its quality.

I am indebted to the team at Rana Books for their exceptional dedication and hard work in bringing this guide to life. Your professionalism, attention to detail, and commitment to excellence have truly made a difference. Special thanks to the editors, designers, and proofreaders for their meticulous efforts in refining the content and ensuring its clarity and coherence.

I would also like to express my gratitude to the educators and experts in the field of PTE preparation who have shared their knowledge and insights. Your expertise has enriched the content of this guide and provided valuable perspectives on achieving success in the PTE exam.

I am immensely grateful to the individuals who have generously shared their experiences and testimonials, adding real-life perspectives and inspiration to this guide. Your willingness to contribute has made this book more relatable and meaningful to future test-takers.

Last but not least, I want to extend my heartfelt thanks to the readers and test-takers who will embark on their PTE preparation journey with this guide. Your dedication, commitment, and trust in this resource are greatly appreciated. It is my sincere hope that "The Ultimate Guide to Excelling in PTE" will serve as a valuable companion on your path to achieving top scores.

To everyone who has contributed in any way to the creation of this guide, thank you from the bottom of my heart. Your support and involvement have been instrumental in making this endeavor a reality.

Sincerely,

Amanpreet Kaur
Author

1

Introduction

Introduction

The Pearson Test of English (PTE) is an internationally recognized English language proficiency exam conducted by Pearson Language Tests. It assesses the English language skills of non-native speakers who wish to study, work, or migrate to English-speaking countries. In this section, we will provide an overview of the PTE Exam, discuss its test format and structure, and explain the scoring criteria and grading system.

1.1 Overview of the PTE Exam

The PTE Exam measures the four key language skills: listening, reading, speaking, and writing. It is a computer-based test that evaluates a candidate's English proficiency through a series of tasks and questions designed to simulate real-life situations.

The exam is divided into three main parts: Speaking and Writing, Reading, and Listening. Each part consists of several sections that assess different language skills. The entire test takes approximately three hours to complete.

1.2 Test Format and Structure

1.2.1 Speaking and Writing

The Speaking and Writing section of the PTE Exam evaluates your ability to communicate effectively in spoken and written English. It includes the following tasks:

- Personal Introduction: You will be asked to introduce yourself within a given time limit.
- Read Aloud: You will have to read a short text aloud.
- Repeat Sentence: You will listen to a sentence and then repeat it accurately.
- Describe Image: You will be shown an image and asked to describe it in detail.
- Re-tell Lecture: You will listen to a lecture and then summarize it in your own words.
- Answer Short Questions: You will answer questions based on brief spoken or recorded prompts.
- Summarize Written Text: You will read a passage and summarize it in a single sentence.
- Essay Writing: You will be given a prompt and required to write an essay in response.

1.2.2 Reading

The Reading section assesses your reading comprehension skills. It includes various question types such as multiple-choice, reorder paragraphs, and fill in the blanks. You will be presented with passages from academic texts, articles, and general interest sources. The tasks will evaluate your ability to understand main ideas, supporting details, vocabulary, and logical relationships within the text.

1.2.3 Listening

The Listening section measures your ability to understand spoken English in academic and everyday contexts. You will listen to a range of audio recordings, including lectures, conversations, and interviews. The tasks include multiple-choice questions, summarize spoken text, fill in the blanks, and highlight correct summary.

1.3 Scoring Criteria and Grading System

The PTE Exam is scored based on a detailed and automated scoring system. Each task is assessed by artificial intelligence technology that evaluates various aspects of your performance.

The scoring system is divided into communicative skills and enabling skills. Communicative skills consist of listening, reading, speaking, and writing, while enabling skills include grammar, oral fluency, pronunciation, spelling, vocabulary, and written discourse.

The overall score is reported on a scale of 10-90 points. Each communicative skill and enabling skill is scored on a scale of 10-90 as well. The score report also provides an indication of your performance level, ranging from "Below proficient" to

"Expert."

In conclusion, the PTE Exam is a comprehensive assessment of your English language proficiency, covering listening, reading, speaking, and writing skills. Understanding the test format, structure, and scoring criteria can help you prepare effectively and perform well on the exam.

2

Preparation Strategies

Preparation Strategies

1. Understand the Test Format: Familiarize yourself with the format of the PTE exam. Understand the sections, question types, time limits, and scoring criteria for each section. This will help you plan your preparation effectively.

2. Take a Diagnostic Test: Start by taking a diagnostic test to assess your current English proficiency level and identify your strengths and weaknesses. This will help you tailor your study plan and allocate more time to areas that need improvement.

3. Study the Test Content: Get familiar with the content that will be tested in each section. Study grammar rules, vocabulary, and common idiomatic expressions. Review academic vocabulary that is commonly used in the test.

4. Practice Regularly: Regular practice is crucial for success in the PTE exam. Set aside dedicated study time each day to practice different sections of the test. Use official PTE practice materials, sample questions, and mock tests to simulate the exam environment.

5. Develop Time Management Skills: The PTE exam is time-bound, so it's important to develop good time management skills. Practice answering questions within the allocated time for each section. Identify strategies to help you quickly and effectively respond to different question types.

6. Improve Reading Skills: Work on improving your reading speed and comprehension. Practice reading academic texts from a variety of sources, such as newspapers, magazines, and online articles. Focus on understanding the main ideas, supporting details, and the author's tone.

7. Enhance Listening Skills: Listen to a wide range of English audio materials, including lectures, podcasts, and news broadcasts. Practice summarizing the main points, identifying key details, and understanding different accents and speech patterns.

8. Enhance Speaking Skills: Practice speaking English regularly. Engage in conversations with native English speakers or language partners. Work on pronunciation, fluency, and coherence. Familiarize yourself with the speaking tasks in the PTE exam and practice responding to them.

9. Improve Writing Skills: Develop your writing skills by practicing different types of essays, summaries, and reports.

Focus on organizing your ideas, using appropriate vocabulary and grammar, and proofreading your work for errors.

10. Use Authentic Resources: Utilize authentic PTE preparation materials and resources. These resources are specifically designed to help you understand the test format and provide targeted practice for each section.

11. Seek Professional Guidance: Consider enrolling in a PTE preparation course or working with a tutor who specializes in PTE coaching. They can provide guidance, feedback, and personalized strategies to improve your performance.

12. Review and Evaluate: Regularly review your progress and evaluate your performance. Identify areas where you need more practice and focus your efforts on improving those areas.

2.1 Defining Your Score Target:

Defining your score target is an important step in preparing for the PTE (Pearson Test of English) exam. It helps you set a clear objective and focus your efforts on achieving that goal. Here's how you can define your score target:

1. Research score requirements: Check the score requirements of the institutions or organizations you are applying to. Different programs or countries may have different score thresholds. This information will give you an idea of the score you need to aim for.

2. Assess your current English proficiency: Take a practice PTE exam or a sample test to assess your current proficiency level. This will help you understand your strengths and weaknesses and give you a baseline score to work with.

3. Consider the validity period: Some institutions have a validity period for PTE scores. Ensure that you set a target score that remains valid throughout your application process.

4. Determine your strengths and weaknesses: Identify the areas in which you are strong and the areas that need improvement. This will help you allocate your study time more effectively and focus on the sections that require more attention.

5. Set a realistic target: Consider your time constraints, study resources, and the difficulty level of the exam. Set a target score that challenges you but is also realistic and attainable within your circumstances.

2.2 Developing a Realistic Study Schedule:

Once you have defined your score target, it's crucial to create a study schedule that allows you to allocate sufficient time to prepare for the PTE exam. Here are some steps to develop a realistic study schedule:

1. Determine your available study time: Assess your daily and weekly schedule to identify the time slots you can dedicate to studying. Consider your work, school, and personal commitments to find suitable study periods.

2. Break down the sections: Divide the PTE exam into its

different sections, such as Speaking, Writing, Reading, and Listening. Determine how much time you need to allocate to each section based on your strengths and weaknesses.

3. Prioritize your weak areas: Allocate more study time to the sections or skills that you struggle with the most. This will help you improve and achieve a balanced overall score.

4. Create a study plan: Break down your study time into smaller, manageable tasks. Set specific goals for each study session, such as completing a practice test, working on vocabulary, or practicing speaking skills.

5. Be consistent: Consistency is key to effective preparation. Spread out your study sessions evenly throughout the week and avoid cramming all the studying into a few days. Regular practice will help you retain information and improve your skills steadily.

6. Allow time for review and practice: Schedule regular review sessions to revisit previously covered material and reinforce your learning. Practice regularly with mock tests to familiarize yourself with the exam format and improve your time management.

7. Be flexible: Be open to adjusting your study schedule if needed. Life events or unforeseen circumstances may require you to adapt your plan. Flexibility will help you maintain a consistent study routine without feeling overwhelmed.

Remember, a realistic study schedule is one that suits your

individual circumstances and allows you to balance your other commitments effectively. Regular practice, focused study sessions, and dedication will contribute to your success in the PTE exam.

3

Familiarizing Yourself with the Test Content

3.1 Detailed Analysis of Each PTE Section:

The Pearson Test of English (PTE) consists of several sections designed to assess your English language proficiency. Here's a detailed analysis of each section:

1. Speaking & Writing:
   - Speaking: In this section, you will be evaluated on your ability to speak English fluently and accurately. It includes tasks such as reading aloud, describing images, answering short questions, and giving longer speeches on a given topic.
   - Writing: This section assesses your writing skills. You will be required to write responses in academic or general English, summarize written texts, write essays, and interpret information from charts or diagrams.

2. Reading:
   - This section measures your reading comprehension skills.

You will encounter various question types, including multiple-choice, reorder paragraphs, and fill in the blanks. The texts will be sourced from academic and general contexts.

3. Listening:
   - This section evaluates your listening comprehension abilities. You will listen to audio recordings of lectures, discussions, and conversations, and answer questions based on what you heard. Question types include multiple-choice, fill in the blanks, and highlight correct summary.

4. Integrated Skills:
   - This section combines your reading, listening, and writing skills. You will be given a prompt and will have to read a text and listen to a recording related to the prompt. Then, you will write a response that integrates the information from both sources.

3.2 Sample Questions and Practice Exercises:

Here are some sample questions and practice exercises for each PTE section:

1. Speaking & Writing:
   - Sample Speaking Question: Describe the image below in 40 seconds.
   - Sample Writing Exercise: Write an essay discussing the advantages and disadvantages of using technology in education.

2. Reading:
   - Sample Reading Question: Choose the correct option to complete the sentence.

- Sample Reading Exercise: Read a passage about climate change and answer questions related to the information in the text.

3. Listening:
   - Sample Listening Question: Listen to a conversation and answer multiple-choice questions based on the dialogue.
   - Sample Listening Exercise: Listen to a lecture on history and complete a summary of the main points.

4. Integrated Skills:
   - Sample Integrated Skills Question: Read a passage about renewable energy, listen to a discussion on the same topic, and write a summary integrating information from both sources.
   - Sample Integrated Skills Exercise: Listen to a recording about a famous author, read a related text, and write a response comparing the information from both sources.

These samples provide a glimpse of the question types you may encounter in each section. To further practice and familiarize yourself with PTE, consider using official PTE preparation materials, including practice tests and mock exams.

4

Developing Key Skills

Enhancing Your Speaking Skills

'Enhancing your speaking skills in the PTE (Pearson Test of English) requires a focused approach to meet the specific requirements of the test. Here are some strategies to help you improve your speaking skills specifically for the PTE:

1. Familiarize Yourself with the Test Format:

- Understand the different tasks: Familiarize yourself with the various speaking tasks in the PTE, such as Read Aloud, Repeat Sentence, Describe Image, Retell Lecture, Answer Short Questions, and Oral Fluency.

- Study the scoring criteria: Understand how your speaking responses are evaluated in terms of pronunciation, fluency, vocabulary, grammatical range, and content.

2. Develop Pronunciation and Fluency:

- Practice pronunciation: Focus on improving your pronunciation by working on individual sounds, stress, intonation, and word linking. Use resources like pronunciation guides, audio materials, or work with a tutor.
- Enhance fluency: Practice speaking at a comfortable pace, without pauses or hesitations. Work on maintaining a steady flow of speech and use fillers (e.g., well, you know) to give yourself time to think if needed.

3. Expand Your Vocabulary and Collocations:

- Study vocabulary in context: Read a variety of texts and listen to authentic materials to expose yourself to new vocabulary. Pay attention to how words are used in different contexts and practice using them in your own sentences.
- Learn collocations: Focus on common word combinations and phrases to improve your spoken English. Practice using collocations in your responses to make them sound more natural and fluent.

4. Practice Time Management and Structuring Responses:

- Understand task requirements: Read the instructions carefully for each speaking task and make sure you understand what is expected of you. Pay attention to any time limits or specific instructions.
- Plan and structure your responses: Take a few seconds to plan your response before you start speaking. Organize your thoughts and structure your answers with a clear introduction, main points, and a conclusion.
- Use cohesive devices: Connect your ideas using transition words and phrases (e.g., however, moreover, on the other hand)

to create coherence in your responses.

- Practice within the time limits: Practice speaking within the time limits set for each task. Time yourself during practice sessions to ensure you can effectively complete the task within the given timeframe.

5. Seek Feedback and Practice Regularly:

- Record and review your responses: Record yourself practicing the speaking tasks and listen to them critically. Identify areas where you can improve, such as pronunciation, fluency, or vocabulary usage.
- Get feedback from experts: Seek feedback from experienced tutors, teachers, or language partners who can provide insights and suggestions for improvement.
- Regular practice: Dedicate regular time to practice speaking in English. Engage in conversations, join speaking clubs, or participate in mock tests to simulate the test environment.

4.1 Speaking Section Overview:

The speaking section of any language assessment or communication activity evaluates your ability to express yourself orally. It measures various aspects of your speaking skills, such as pronunciation, fluency, vocabulary usage, grammar accuracy, and coherence of your responses. The specific requirements and format may vary depending on the assessment or task, but the following strategies can generally help you enhance your speaking skills.

4.2 Pronunciation and Fluency Improvement:

- Listen and imitate: Pay attention to native speakers and try to imitate their pronunciation and intonation patterns. This will help you develop a more natural-sounding speech.
- Practice regularly: Engage in activities that require speaking, such as conversations with native speakers, language exchange programs, or even reading aloud. Regular practice will help improve your fluency over time.
- Use audio resources: Utilize podcasts, audiobooks, or language learning apps that provide audio materials. Listening to native speakers will help you become more familiar with the natural rhythm and pronunciation of the language.
- Seek feedback: Record yourself speaking and listen to the recordings. Identify areas where you can improve and seek feedback from teachers, language partners, or online communities.

4.3 Building Vocabulary and Collocations:

- Read extensively: Read books, newspapers, online articles, and other materials in the target language. This exposure to different contexts and vocabulary will expand your knowledge and improve your ability to express yourself effectively.
- Use vocabulary-building techniques: Create flashcards, use vocabulary apps, or maintain a vocabulary journal to record new words and review them regularly.
- Learn collocations: Collocations are words that commonly go together. Pay attention to how words are used in phrases or sentences, and try to memorize and use them in context. For example, instead of just learning the word "make," learn common collocations like "make a decision," "make an effort," etc.

- Engage in conversations: Actively participate in conversations with native speakers or language exchange partners. Use new vocabulary and collocations to practice incorporating them into your speech.

4.4 Strategies for Structuring Responses:

- Understand the question/task: Read or listen to the question or prompt carefully, and ensure you understand what is being asked of you. Take note of any key terms or specific instructions.
- Plan your response: Before speaking, take a few seconds to gather your thoughts and outline the main points you want to cover in your response. This will help you organize your ideas and provide a well-structured answer.
- Use introductory phrases: Begin your response with an introductory phrase or sentence that clearly states your main point or opinion. This will give your response coherence and make it easier for the listener to follow your ideas.
- Provide supporting details: Use examples, explanations, or personal experiences to support your main points. This will make your response more engaging and persuasive.
- Use cohesive devices: Employ transition words and phrases (e.g., however, moreover, on the other hand) to connect your ideas and create a smooth flow in your response.
- Monitor your time: Keep track of the time allotted for your response and ensure that you use it wisely. Pace yourself to cover all the necessary points without rushing or going over time.

Remember that practice is key to improving your speaking skills. The more you expose yourself to the target language and actively engage in speaking activities, the more confident and proficient you will become.

5

Improving Your Listening Skills

Improving your listening skills is crucial for success in the PTE (Pearson Test of English) examination. In this context, let's explore each section related to improving your listening abilities in the PTE.

5.1 Listening Section Overview:

The Listening section in the PTE assesses your ability to understand spoken English in academic and everyday contexts. It consists of various question types, such as multiple-choice, highlight correct summary, fill in the blanks, and more. The section aims to evaluate your comprehension skills, including understanding main ideas, details, opinions, and the speaker's purpose.

5.2 Active Listening Techniques:

To excel in the Listening section of the PTE, it's crucial to employ active listening techniques. Here are some strategies to help you become a better active listener during the test:

- Focus attentively: Give your undivided attention to the audio recording. Concentrate on the speaker's words, tone, and emphasis to understand the intended message.

- Anticipate the content: Before the audio starts, quickly scan the question or prompt to have an idea of what to expect. This will help you focus on relevant information during the recording.

- Take effective notes: Develop a shorthand system to jot down key points, keywords, and important details while listening. This will aid in later referencing during the answering phase.

- Engage with the audio: Mentally summarize or paraphrase the speaker's statements to ensure your understanding. Stay actively engaged by predicting what might come next.

5.3 Note-Taking Strategies:

Note-taking plays a vital role in the Listening section of the PTE. Effective note-taking helps you capture essential information and recall it accurately while answering questions. Consider the following strategies:

- Use symbols and abbreviations: Develop a system of symbols and abbreviations to quickly note down information. For example, use arrows for cause-and-effect relationships or asterisks for important points.

- Organize your notes: Use headings, bullet points, or columns to structure your notes. This will make it easier to locate specific information during the answering phase.

- Focus on keywords: Identify keywords that convey the main ideas or key details. Highlight or underline them to quickly locate relevant information later.

5.4 Identifying Key Information and Understanding Context:

In the Listening section, it's important to identify key information and understand the context to answer questions accurately. Consider the following tips:

- Pay attention to emphasis: Note when the speaker emphasizes certain words or phrases, as they often indicate important information or opinions.

- Notice transitional words: Words like "however," "therefore," or "consequently" help you understand the relationships between different ideas presented in the audio.

- Understand context clues: Pay attention to the overall context of the recording. The speaker's tone, background sounds, or accompanying visuals (if applicable) can provide valuable hints to comprehend the information better.

- Infer meaning: Sometimes, the speaker may not explicitly state certain information. In such cases, use your inference skills to understand implied meanings or draw conclusions based on the given context.

Improving your listening skills in the PTE requires practice and familiarity with the test format. By employing active listening techniques, effective note-taking strategies, and understanding the context, you can enhance your performance and achieve better results in the Listening section of the PTE.

6

Mastering Your Reading Skills

6.1 Reading Section Overview:

The Reading section in the PTE (Pearson Test of English) evaluates your ability to comprehend written texts and answer questions based on them. This section assesses your reading skills, including your understanding of main ideas, supporting details, vocabulary, and inference abilities. It consists of multiple-choice questions, reorder paragraphs, and fill in the blanks tasks.

6.2 Speed Reading Techniques:

Speed reading techniques can help you improve your reading speed and efficiency. Here are a few strategies you can use:

1. Eliminate subvocalization: Subvocalization is the habit of pronouncing words silently in your mind as you read. By reducing or eliminating this habit, you can read faster. Practice by consciously focusing on reading without vocalizing the words.

2. Avoid regression: Regression is the tendency to go back and reread words or sentences. Train yourself to read forward without going back to previous sections unless necessary.

3. Expand your visual span: Rather than focusing on individual words, try to expand your vision to take in groups of words or phrases at once. This can help you process information more quickly.

4. Use a pacer: A pacer is an object (e.g., a pen, finger, or cursor) that you move along the text as you read. It helps maintain a steady reading pace and prevents regression.

5. Practice with timed exercises: Set a timer and challenge yourself to read a passage within a specific time frame. Gradually reduce the time as you improve to increase your reading speed.

Remember, while speed is important, comprehension should not be compromised. Maintain a balance between speed and understanding the text.

6.3 Skimming and Scanning Strategies:

Skimming and scanning are techniques that allow you to quickly locate information within a text. They are particularly useful when you have limited time to read and answer questions. Here's how you can use these strategies effectively:

Skimming:

- Read the title, headings, and subheadings to get an overview of the text's main ideas.
- Look at the first and last sentence of each paragraph to grasp

the topic and flow of the content.

- Pay attention to bold or italicized words, bullet points, and any emphasized information.
- Read the first and last paragraph in detail to understand the introduction and conclusion.

Scanning:

- Have a clear idea of what you're searching for before you start scanning.
- Run your eyes quickly over the text, focusing on keywords, numbers, or specific information you need.
- Utilize visual cues like headings, subheadings, and formatting styles to locate relevant sections.
- Don't read every word; instead, let your eyes move rapidly across the text to find the specific details you're seeking.

Remember, skimming and scanning are meant to save time, but they may not provide an in-depth understanding of the text. You should switch to more detailed reading when necessary, especially for answering specific questions that require comprehension of the content.

By practicing speed reading techniques, skimming, and scanning strategies, you can enhance your reading skills and perform better in the Reading section of the PTE. Regular practice and exposure to various types of texts will also contribute to your overall reading proficiency.

7

Excelling in Writing Tasks

7.1 Writing Section Overview:

The Writing section in the PTE (Pearson Test of English) assesses your ability to effectively convey ideas in written form. It consists of two tasks: Summarize Written Text and Write Essay. The section evaluates your skills in grammar, vocabulary, coherence, cohesion, and overall writing proficiency.

7.2 Essay Writing Tips and Approaches:

When approaching the essay writing task in the PTE, consider the following tips:

1. Understand the prompt: Read the essay prompt carefully and make sure you understand what is being asked. Identify the key points and determine the purpose and scope of your essay.

2. Plan your essay: Take a few minutes to brainstorm and outline your ideas before starting to write. Organize your thoughts and create a clear structure for your essay, including an introduction, body paragraphs, and a conclusion.

3. Focus on one main idea per paragraph: Each body paragraph should present and develop a single main idea or argument. Support your ideas with relevant examples, evidence, or explanations.

4. Use a variety of sentence structures and vocabulary: Demonstrate your language skills by using a range of sentence structures and vocabulary. Avoid repetitive words or phrases and aim for clarity and precision in your writing.

5. Maintain coherence and cohesion: Ensure that your ideas flow logically from one paragraph to the next. Use appropriate transition words and phrases to connect your sentences and paragraphs smoothly.

6. Manage your time effectively: Allocate enough time for planning, writing, and reviewing your essay. Keep an eye on the clock to ensure you complete your essay within the given time limit.

7.3 Summarizing Written Text:

The Summarize Written Text task requires you to write a concise summary of a given text. Here are some tips to excel in this task:

- Read the passage carefully and identify the main ideas, supporting details, and the overall message.
- Focus on the most important information and leave out less significant details.
- Use your own words to paraphrase and summarize the content effectively.

- Aim for a summary length of 30 to 40 words while ensuring it captures the essence of the passage.
- Check your grammar and spelling to maintain accuracy in your response.

7.4 Constructing Responses with Clarity and Coherence:

To construct responses with clarity and coherence, keep the following points in mind:

- Start with a clear topic sentence that states the main idea of each paragraph.
- Use supporting evidence, examples, or explanations to develop your main points.
- Ensure a logical flow of ideas by using appropriate transition words and phrases.
- Check for coherence in your writing by reviewing the overall structure and organization of your essay or response.
- Revise and edit your work for grammar, punctuation, and spelling errors to maintain clarity and accuracy.

Practice writing essays and summarizing texts within the given time constraints. Seek feedback from others or utilize online resources to improve your writing skills. Regular practice and attention to detail will help you excel in the Writing section of the PTE.

8

Test-Taking Strategies

8. Time Management Techniques:

Effective time management is crucial for success in the PTE. Here are some strategies to help you manage your time efficiently during the test:

8.1 Planning Your Time for Each Section:

- Familiarize yourself with the structure of the PTE and the time allocated for each section. This will help you plan your time accordingly.
- Allocate more time to sections that you find challenging or have more questions.
- Divide your time evenly among the questions in each section to ensure you have sufficient time to answer all of them.
- Keep in mind that different sections may require different approaches to time management. For example, the Speaking section requires immediate responses, while the Writing section allows more time for planning and revising.

8.2 Prioritizing Questions and Managing Pacing:

- Read through the instructions and questions quickly at the beginning of each section to get an idea of the task requirements.
- Prioritize questions based on your strengths and the number of points allocated to each question. Focus on questions that you are confident about and can answer quickly.
- If you encounter a difficult question, don't spend too much time on it. Mark it and move on to the next question. You can come back to it later if you have time.
- Manage your pacing by keeping an eye on the time and the number of questions remaining. Avoid spending too much time on a single question or section, as it may affect your performance in other parts of the test.
- Use shortcuts and strategies to save time where applicable. For example, in multiple-choice questions, eliminate obviously incorrect options to narrow down your choices and make an educated guess if necessary.
- Be mindful of the time left in each section and allocate a few minutes at the end to review your answers, especially for sections with multiple-choice questions or where you have time for revisions.

Practice time management during your test preparation by simulating the test environment and setting time limits for each section. This will help you become familiar with the pacing required and improve your efficiency on test day.

9

Dealing with Test Anxiety and Stress

Test anxiety and stress are common challenges faced by many students, including those taking the PTE (Pearson Test of English). To effectively manage exam stress and perform at your best, it's important to employ strategies for managing stress and incorporate relaxation techniques into your preparation. Here are some strategies and techniques to help you deal with test anxiety and stress in the PTE:

9.1 Strategies for Managing Exam Stress:

1. Start Early: Begin your preparation well in advance of the test date. Procrastination can contribute to increased stress levels. Give yourself enough time to study and review the test material thoroughly.

2. Create a Study Plan: Develop a structured study plan that outlines what you need to cover each day. Breaking down the material into smaller, manageable tasks can make the preparation process less overwhelming and help you stay organized.

3. Set Realistic Goals: Set realistic and achievable goals for each study session. This will give you a sense of accomplishment and motivate you to continue working towards your objectives. Avoid setting unrealistic expectations that can lead to unnecessary stress.

4. Practice Time Management: Effective time management is crucial during the exam. Familiarize yourself with the different sections of the PTE and allocate specific time slots for each. Regularly practice timed mock tests to improve your pacing and ensure you complete each section within the allocated time.

5. Take Breaks: Incorporate regular breaks into your study routine. Studying for long periods without breaks can lead to mental fatigue and increased stress levels. Short breaks can help you recharge and maintain focus.

6. Seek Support: Don't hesitate to reach out to friends, family, or fellow test-takers for support. Sharing your concerns and experiences can provide emotional support and help alleviate anxiety. Consider joining study groups or online forums where you can discuss PTE-related topics and learn from others.

9.2 Relaxation Techniques and Mental Preparation:

1. Deep Breathing: Practice deep breathing exercises to help calm your mind and body. Take slow, deep breaths, hold for a few seconds, and then exhale slowly. Deep breathing can trigger the relaxation response and reduce anxiety.

2. Progressive Muscle Relaxation: This technique involves tensing and releasing each muscle group in your body to promote

relaxation. Start from your toes and work your way up to your head, consciously tensing and then releasing each muscle group.

3. Visualization: Use visualization techniques to imagine yourself in a calm and confident state during the exam. Visualize successfully completing each section, answering questions with ease, and achieving your desired score. This can help build positive associations and reduce anxiety.

4. Positive Affirmations: Repeat positive affirmations to yourself before and during the exam. Affirmations such as "I am well-prepared," "I can handle this test," or "I am confident in my abilities" can boost your self-belief and help you stay calm under pressure.

5. Healthy Lifestyle: Prioritize self-care by maintaining a healthy lifestyle. Get regular exercise, eat nutritious meals, and ensure you get enough sleep. Physical well-being has a significant impact on your mental state and can help reduce stress.

6. Mock Tests and Simulations: Familiarize yourself with the PTE format by practicing with mock tests and simulations. The more you expose yourself to the test environment, the more comfortable you will become, reducing anxiety on the actual test day.

Remember that managing test anxiety and stress is a gradual process. Implement these strategies and techniques consistently, and you'll likely experience improvements in your ability to cope with exam-related stress. Practice self-compassion and believe in your abilities. Good luck with your PTE preparation!

10

Mock Tests and Practice Drills

10.1 Importance of Mock Tests:

Mock tests are essential for effective preparation in the PTE. They provide numerous benefits, including:

1. Familiarity with the test format: Mock tests allow you to become familiar with the structure, instructions, and types of questions in the PTE. This familiarity reduces anxiety and helps you navigate through the actual test smoothly.

2. Time management practice: Mock tests simulate the time constraints of the actual exam, allowing you to practice managing your time effectively for each section. This helps you develop pacing strategies and ensure that you can complete all sections within the allotted time.

3. Identifying strengths and weaknesses: Mock tests help you identify your strong areas and areas that require improvement. By analyzing your performance in different sections, you can

focus your study efforts on the areas where you need more practice.

4. Building test-taking strategies: Through mock tests, you can experiment with different test-taking strategies and techniques. You can learn how to approach different question types, prioritize questions, and manage your responses efficiently.

5. Building confidence: Regularly taking mock tests builds your confidence and reduces test-related stress. It familiarizes you with the test environment, allowing you to feel more comfortable and focused during the actual exam.

10.2 Simulating Test Conditions:

To derive the maximum benefit from mock tests, it's important to simulate test conditions as closely as possible. Here are some tips to create a realistic test environment:

1. Set aside dedicated time: Allocate specific blocks of time for mock tests, just as you would for the actual exam. Choose a quiet and distraction-free environment to replicate the test conditions.

2. Use official practice materials: Utilize official PTE practice materials, including sample tests or practice exams, to ensure that you are exposed to authentic questions and content.

3. Follow test instructions strictly: Adhere to the instructions and guidelines provided for each section. Practice answering questions within the time limits specified for each task.

4. Use the required tools: Familiarize yourself with the digital tools used in the PTE, such as the microphone for the Speaking section or the text editor for the Writing section. Practice using these tools during your mock tests.

5. Avoid distractions: Minimize external distractions during the mock tests. Turn off your phone, avoid interruptions, and create a quiet environment to simulate the focus required during the actual exam.

10.3 Analyzing Results and Identifying Weak Areas:

After completing mock tests, it's crucial to analyze your performance to identify your weak areas and areas that require improvement. Here's how you can do it effectively:

1. Review your answers: Go through each section and question, reviewing both the correct and incorrect answers. Understand the reasoning behind the correct responses and learn from any mistakes you made.

2. Identify patterns: Look for patterns in your incorrect answers or areas where you struggled consistently. This could indicate specific skills or question types that you need to work on.

3. Seek feedback: If possible, have a knowledgeable person, such as a teacher or tutor, review your performance and provide feedback. They can offer insights and suggest strategies to address your weaknesses.

4. Create a study plan: Based on your analysis, create a study

plan that focuses on improving your weak areas. Allocate more time to practice and revise the topics or question types that you struggled with the most.

5. Retake mock tests periodically: Regularly retake mock tests to track your progress and assess the effectiveness of your study plan. Use the results to adjust your strategies and continue improving.

Mock tests and practice drills should be an integral part of your PTE preparation. By simulating test conditions, analyzing your results, and targeting your weak areas, you can enhance your performance and increase your chances of success in the actual exam.

www.ingramcontent.com/pod-product-compliance
Ingram Content Group UK Ltd.
Pitfield, Milton Keynes, MK11 3LW, UK
UKHW021934190726
13853UKWH00004B/1433

9 798394 654831